The Tempest

William Shakespeare

Retold by
Teesta Guha Sarkar

SCHOLASTIC
New York Toronto London Auckland
Sydney New Delhi Hong Kong

Published by Scholastic India Pvt. Ltd.
A subsidiary of Scholastic Inc., New York, 10012 (USA).
Publishers since 1920, with international operations in Canada, Australia, New Zealand, the United Kingdom, India, and Hong Kong.

For information regarding permission, write to:
Scholastic India Pvt. Ltd.
Golf View Corporate Tower-A, 3rd Floor,
DLF Phase V, Gurgaon 122002 (India)

First edition: May 2012
Reprint: September 2018 Dec2025

ISBN-13: 978-81-8477-092-6

Printed at Ram Printograph, Delhi

The Lexile measure of this book (980L) represents the complexity of the text. This Lexile measure—along with other characteristics of the text, such as developmental level and subject matter—helps in selecting books that best match a reader's level and goals. For more information on using Lexile measures to connect readers with text, visit www.Lexile.com.

Contents

Characters

Prospero: *the rightful Duke of Milan*

Antonio: *his brother, the usurping Duke of Milan*

Alonso: *King of Naples*

Sebastian: *his brother*

Miranda: *daughter to Prospero*

Caliban: *slave to Prospero*

Ferdinand: *son to Alonso*

Gonzalo: *a councillor*

Adrian and Francisco: *lords*

Trinculo: *a jester*

Stephano: *a drunken butler*

Master: *of a ship*

Boatswain

Mariners

Ariel: *an airy spirit*

Iris, Ceres, Juno, Nymphs, Reapers: *spirits*

1

The ill-fated ship was out at sea. It had on board some of the most august personages from Italy—King Alonso of Naples, Sebastian his brother, Ferdinand his son, and Antonio the Duke of Milan.

The wedding had gone well, and the king's daughter Claribel was now Queen of Tunis. Alonso quietly mourned her departure from his life, as they sailed on the Mediterranean waters, bound for home. But soon the ship found itself amidst a frightening storm. Tempestuous noises surrounded the passengers, lightning rent the ominous sky.

'Boatswain!' the shipmaster cried. 'Speak to the mariners; tell them what needs to be done. Hurry, or the ship runs aground!'

Without wasting any time the boatswain gave instructions to the crew, shouted words of encouragement, and threw a challenge, albeit an empty one, to the obstinate storm.

Alonso and a part of his entourage had come out to the deck in order to take stock of the situation. Afraid and angry, they questioned the boatswain's expertise and hurled accusations at him.

'Where's the master, boatswain?' Antonio demanded impatiently.

The boatswain knew that the roaring waves would make no discrimination between commoner and king, but drown everyone alike. So he paid no heed to Antonio—the boatswain was not one to cower to his interfering commands.

'Return to your cabins,' he said firmly to the passengers on deck. 'You keep us from our work with your pointless talk.'

The old councillor Gonzalo warned him to not be so brusque with the king and his men. But the boatswain declared that he cared for no one more than he did for himself, and if Gonzalo could silence the elements and restore peace and calm, he would command the mariners to stop work immediately. This Gonzalo could not do, so 'Out of our way, I say,' the boatswain yelled to him and his party.

Taking note of the boatswain's complexion, Gonzalo remarked that he was certainly born to be hanged and not to die at sea. So he argued that the passengers could come to no harm if the boatswain himself would not drown.

In the meantime the storm continued to rage, making it impossible for the mariners to control the ship. Cries of frustration could be heard from the cabins, and once again Antonio appeared, this time accompanied by an angry Sebastian.

'Merciless dog, may you be wracked by disease!' Sebastian

said. Antonio joined in, 'Go hang yourself, you lazy noise-maker!' They were certain that the boatswain's efforts would come to nothing.

While Gonzalo tried to placate the two men, the boatswain turned a deaf ear to their insults, and instructed his mariners to drive the ship out to open sea again. It had come so close to an island that it was in danger of crashing on its shore.

The mariners had lost all hope. 'To prayers, to prayers!' they cried. But the hardy boatswain would not acknowledge defeat. As he continued to struggle against the storm, Antonio suggested they all sink with the king, the boatswain's efforts having failed completely. More confused noises came from the cabins as despairing passengers bade farewell to their wife and children. But Gonzalo continued to be optimistic in the face of all the chaos. 'The wills above be done, but I would gladly die on land,' he said, as the ship battled the monstrous waves.

***

On the island at whose shore the ship would finally come to rest, the young Miranda was pleading with her father. She had seen the passengers suffer as the tempest threatened to sink the vessel, and her heart had gone out to them. 'If you are indeed capable of such powers, let the storm abate, dear father,' she said to Prospero. Thinking that every person on the ship had perished, Miranda wished she could have sunk the sea within the earth before it swallowed the ship and its helpless passengers.

But she was mistaken. 'No one has come to any harm,' Prospero told her. 'Everything I have done today has been for your benefit, my daughter, unaware as you are of your origins, and that your father was once more than just a master of a humble home on an uncharted island.'

'It is time you found out who you are, and the reason for the tempest I have brought about today,' continued Prospero. 'The wreck which moved your heart to such great compassion I have carefully arranged by the use of my magical powers. You may have heard the wretched souls cry, but I can assure you that they have lost not even a hair today.'

Surprised by Prospero's explanation, Miranda sat down to listen attentively to her father as he began to relate the story of their past.

'Do you remember a time before we came to this island?' Prospero asked. 'But how can that be—you were only three then.'

'I do remember, father,' replied Miranda. 'My memories seem like dreams and do not serve as assurance, but were there not several women once who looked after me?'

There certainly were—Prospero told her—twelve years ago, when he was Duke of Milan, and father to Miranda, the only child born to him and his virtuous wife.

'It was my brother Antonio's foul play that compelled

us to leave Milan,' Prospero explained. 'But on our way out, we received much help from those who still cared for us.'

He recounted his love for his brother, a love which Antonio had returned with nothing but treason. Immersed in the study of the liberal arts, Prospero had entrusted his brother with the management of the state, and become a stranger to his own dukedom. Seeing an opportunity for overthrowing his brother, Antonio quickly learnt how to manipulate his officials into going against Prospero.

Unaware of the treachery that was under way, Prospero neglected all worldly duties and dedicated himself to the improvement of his mind, allowing Antonio's evil nature ample time to flourish. This treacherous brother began to enjoy not only the revenue of his office but also the rewards won by means of his newfound position. Deluded by the power he had unlawfully acquired, Antonio began to think himself the rightful Duke of Milan, and his ambition grew unbounded.

He knew full well of the long-standing enmity between his brother and the King of Naples. So Antonio offered the king a handsome tribute and undue homage, in return for which he asked for Milan to be conferred upon him, and that Prospero be deported from the dukedom. So at the midnight hour on the fateful night were father and daughter pushed out of the gates of Milan by several malicious ministers appointed for the purpose.

'But why did they not destroy us?' asked Miranda.

They dared not—Prospero explained—as that would reveal their true motives to one and all; they painted their foul ends a fairer colour instead. The ministers had hurried the outcasts onto a decrepit boat that had neither tackle nor sail nor mast, and left them with nothing to do but helplessly cry to the sea and the winds. There was indeed no hope in sight, but with Miranda by his side, like a beautiful angel, Prospero had felt infused with the strength to face the difficulties that lay ahead.

But they were not completely high and dry; the noble Gonzalo had secretly furnished Prospero with food and water, garments and other amenities. The kind minister had even brought Prospero several books from his library, which he knew his master prized above his dukedom. With these provisions at hand, they travelled on foreign waters till they reached the shores of an unknown island. 'And on this island have I been your schoolmaster,' said Prospero, 'and from my lessons you have made more profit than vain princes can ever hope to from what their careless tutors can offer.'

Miranda expressed her heartfelt gratitude, but also reminded her father that she was yet to be apprised of the reason for the dreadful storm. 'There isn't time,' Prospero told her. 'Cease further questions, as an auspicious star now shines on me, and I must make the most of my fortunes immediately lest they start to droop again.'

Getting up abruptly, Prospero called for his servant Ariel to show himself. Then by his sleight of hand he caused his daughter to feel an overwhelming drowsiness. And before long, Miranda was sleeping soundly.

By this time Ariel arrived and described to his master's satisfaction how he had roused the tempest and made the waves tremble, causing shock on deck and in every cabin, exactly as Prospero had bade him do. Prospero congratulated the spirit for performing the tasks impressively, but asked if the shipwrecked passengers were safe.

'Not a hair out of place,' informed Ariel, 'not even a blemish has marred their garments. I have followed every order you gave, and dispersed the people in groups all over the island. All but Ferdinand, the king's son, who I have left by himself at a corner of the isle, where he is sitting even now, his arms folded in a sad knot.' The king's ship was safe too, hidden away in a nook, where Ariel had charmed the mariners into a deep sleep.

It was already past noon. The hours between then and six were to be used valuably. But before he resumed duties, Ariel reminded his master of the reward he had promised. 'For the constant toils I have performed at your behest, you owe me my liberty.' But Prospero did not take kindly to this demand. 'Ill-humoured servant! You make too much of the tasks you have performed. Do you forget the torment I freed you from?' he said.

Years ago, several acts of sorcery had caused Sycorax to be banished from the city of Algiers. She and Caliban, her son, had been left on this island by sailors. Sycorax had then employed Ariel to do her bidding, who was too delicate to perform the earthy tasks she would set him. He had refused, and in a fit of mad rage, Sycorax had imprisoned him in a tree. There he remained for twelve years, till Prospero came to live on the island, heard his desperate howls for help and set him free.

'If you continue to complain,' Prospero threatened, 'I will fasten you with a peg inside an oak tree and let you howl away for twelve more winters.' So Ariel begged his master's pardon and promised to be more submissive; it was only two more days till Prospero would grant him his freedom after all. Then he left to turn himself into a water nymph and become invisible to all but himself and Prospero.

It was time to pay Caliban a visit. So Prospero awoke Miranda, who said she wasn't keen on laying eyes on their hateful slave. But her father reminded her that they could not do without him either. 'He makes our fire, fetches us wood, and performs other tasks that benefit us greatly.'

Outside Caliban's cave, Ariel appeared as a nymph, in whose ear Prospero whispered further instructions. In the meantime Caliban emerged, greeting father and daughter now above me.' He continued to walk, hoping to find the source of this magical sound.

Ariel had led Ferdinand on to where Prospero was waiting with Miranda. He asked his daughter to open her eyes as Ferdinand walked in their direction.

Miranda gasped. 'A handsome spirit!' she said. But no, he was only human, much like themselves—her father explained—a survivor of the shipwreck, filled with grief and looking for his companions from whom he had got separated.

But he was a thing divine in Miranda's eyes; never before had she seen anyone as noble as Ferdinand. It pleased Prospero to see his daughter so enamoured of the king's son; this was his design after all.

Ferdinand too was awe-struck by Miranda's beauty, and took her to be the island's goddess, on whom he thought the musical spirits attended. 'Grant my prayer,' he said to her, 'for some instruction as to how one must conduct himself on this island. And my last question—are you human too like me?'

'I am, sir,' she replied. 'You mistake me for a wonder.'

Surprised to hear her speak his tongue, he informed Miranda that of all those who spoke this language he was the highest in rank. Believing his father to have drowned, Ferdinand thought he was now King of Naples.

'How the highest?' Prospero joined the conversation.

'What if the King of Naples heard you?'

Surprised once again, this time to hear Prospero speak of Naples, Ferdinand told him of his father's death in a shipwreck, which had also taken the lives of all his friends, the Duke of Milan and his brave son included.

'The Duke of Milan and his braver daughter would rebuke you this moment if only the time was right,' Prospero thought, annoyed by Ferdinand's reference to Antonio as the duke.

But Miranda wasn't upset in the least. What troubled her though was the ungentle way in which Prospero spoke to Ferdinand. When he expressed his desire to make her Queen of Naples, Prospero accused him of being an impostor who had come to the island to try and win it from its master. But Miranda protested, 'Nothing ill can dwell in a form so beautiful!'

Ignoring her remonstrations, Prospero proceeded to chain Ferdinand hand and foot. Ferdinand drew his sword in an attempt to resist, but Prospero wielded his magic staff and charmed him from moving.

'Have pity, father,' Miranda pleaded. But Prospero would not let his daughter and Ferdinand unite so easily. He intended to put obstacles in their path so they would find each other even more valuable than they already did.

'Silence!' he said to Miranda. 'One word more and I will rebuke you. You are a foolish girl for thinking that there are no other men like him, having only Caliban for comparison.'

This did not matter to Miranda, for she had no desire to see a better man. And imprisonment would not affect him one bit—Ferdinand said—if only he could see Miranda once a day from his cell.

'As free as the mountain winds you shall be,' Prospero whispered to the invisible Ariel, seeing that his plans were on the path to success. Then he ordered Ferdinand, with his hands in shackles, to follow him.

2

'Please be merry, sir,' said Gonzalo. He and the other lords had found themselves on an unknown island after the shipwreck, on which they now quibbled with one another.

It was the same island of which Prospero was master, but they knew nothing of his design—that his manoeuvre had brought them there, that not a single soul had perished in the storm. So Gonzalo made attempts at consolation. 'It is common for the masters of ships to suffer the loss that we have suffered. But as for our miraculous preservation, there is nothing as rare. And that is why, good sir, you must weigh your sorrow with your comfort.'

It was only with cynicism that Antonio and Sebastian responded to the garrulous councillor.

'Look, he's winding up the watch of his wit. Let the next auspicious hour strike, and we will hear him utter another witticism,' said Sebastian.

'Sir—' Gonzalo began.

'It has struck one. Tell,' Sebastian quipped.

'For every grief that is entertained, comes to the entertainer—'

'A dollar,' said Sebastian, cutting Gonzalo short.

'Dolour comes to him indeed,' Gonzalo remarked, punning on the cynical lord's comment. 'Therefore, my lord—'

'Oh how lavishly he uses his tongue!' Antonio complained, and Gonzalo was once again interrupted.

'Now who do you think will speak first?' Antonio asked the king's brother, and suggested they make a bet. 'Adrian or Gonzalo?'

'The old cock,' Sebastian said, referring to the old councillor.

'The cockerel,' said Antonio, meaning the young Adrian.

'And what will our wager be?' Sebastian asked.

'A laughter,' said Antonio.

It was Adrian who spoke first. 'Though this island seems deserted …'

'Ha ha ha.' Antonio had won the bet.

They now listened to the lord as he shared his thoughts. '… yet it has a tender, delicate air.' Gonzalo was in agreement. So luscious was the grass that it certainly looked like life could flourish there with ease. What was unusual though—he pointed out—was that their garments, instead of being ruined by the salty water, were dry and glossy, and looked as fresh as the time they had put them on in Africa, when the king's daughter Claribel got married to the Tunisian king.

'Not since widow Dido's time was Tunis graced by such an incomparable queen,' said Gonzalo.

'Widow Dido?' Adrian wanted to make sure. 'She was from Carthage, not Tunis,' he informed his audience.

'Tunis wasn't so different from Carthage then,' Gonzalo said, harking back to the time when Carthage was destroyed, and Tunis took its place as the commercial centre of the region.

Gonzalo and Adrian thus engaged in conversation again, gave their cynical listeners another opportunity to bandy words with them.

'Gonzalo's words are more powerful than Amphion's harp that raised the city of Thebes,' began Antonio. 'What impossible feat will he achieve next?'

'I think he will carry this island home in his pocket, like he would an apple, and gift it to his son,' said Sebastian.

'Then he will sow its kernels in the sea and produce more islands,' Antonio continued.

'But sir,' Gonzalo said to Alonso, reminding everyone of what was originally being discussed, 'do our clothes not seem as fresh as when we were at Tunis, attending your daughter's wedding?'

'You cram more words into my ears than I can bear at this time,' complained Alonso. He had not recovered even a little from the pain he suffered, thinking his son was lost to the sea, and his daughter to Tunis, a city so far removed from Italy that he feared he would never see her again.

Alonso's despair filled Lord Francisco with sympathy. He had kept out of the conversation all this while, but now felt urged to comfort the king. 'I saw your brave son push the waves down and ride on their backs,' said Francisco. 'He flung the hostile waters aside, and his bold head was always above the surges, and soon he reached the base of a wave-worn cliff. I have no doubt that he reached land shortly after.'

But no amount of consolation could change Alonso's mind. 'My son's gone,' he insisted.

'And only you are to blame for this terrible state of affairs,' said Sebastian. 'Everyone pleaded with you, your fair daughter included, to not marry her to a king in a land so distant. Now we have lost not only her, but your son too, on our journey back from his sister's wedding. Had you listened to us, this journey would not have taken place at all.'

The time of course was not right for Alonso to face these difficult truths. Full of pity for his grieving king, Gonzalo suggested that Sebastian be gentler in his criticism. 'Very well,' Sebastian finally conceded.

Having brought an end to this unpleasantness, the councillor began meditating on a new subject: how he would govern the island if he were its master. Ignoring Antonio and Sebastian's foolish remarks that quickly followed, Gonzalo declared that he would not follow custom, but on this island allow no business or sophisticated education, no employment of servants, no boundaries separating one piece of land from another, no farming and husbandry—in short, no occupation whatsoever. It would be an island of idle men and women, and yet they would remain innocent and pure, proving wrong all those who believed that idleness begets lust. There would be no sovereignty on it either.

'Still he would be its sovereign,' Sebastian pointed out on hearing this last remark.

'He seems to have forgotten that he declared himself master of the island,' Antonio said in agreement.

Alonso, still in mourning, felt disturbed by Gonzalo's ramblings. 'I request you to stop,' he told the councillor.

'And stop I will, your majesty,' said Gonzalo. 'These gentlemen needed an opportunity for laughter, and that is what I provided them. They are men of nimble lungs, and it takes little provocation to drive them to laugh at nothing.'

'We were laughing at you,' Antonio said defensively.

'Since you treat me like a person of no significance, I must be nothing to you,' said Gonzalo. 'So you may continue to laugh at nothing if you please.'

'What a blow he has given,' Antonio said sarcastically, having run out of arguments.

While the men continued to banter, Ariel arrived, playing a soporific tune. As if on cue, Gonzalo's lids grew heavy, and he fell asleep momentarily. The lords followed suit.

'I wish my eyes would shut too, and thereby put an end to my morbid thoughts,' said Alonso. And no sooner had he voiced his wish than sleep came to his eyes as well. 'We will guard your person while you rest,' Antonio promised, as he watched Alonso succumb to his sudden drowsiness. But Antonio soon revealed to his friend that he did not mean to keep his word.

'You see, Sebastian,' he said, 'they all fell together as if struck by lightning. How is it that we are not disposed to sleep? But no matter; an opportunity has presented itself, and I see a crown dropping on your head. Do you hear me?'

This suggestion took Sebastian by surprise. 'You seem to be talking in your sleep, Antonio,' he said. 'And such a strange sleep it is—to have your eyes wide open, be standing, speaking, moving, and yet so fast asleep.'

'My noble friend,' Antonio explained, 'it is not me, but your fortune that sleeps. I speak in all seriousness, and you must be serious too, for if you are, you will be three times greater than now.'

'Teach me how to be serious then,' said Sebastian. 'So far I have only been guided by hereditary sloth.'

So Antonio instructed his friend. He pointed to the sleeping Gonzalo, and suggested that when his time would be up not many people would remember him. And although he had insisted that Ferdinand had not survived the shipwreck, it was an idea as implausible as that of the councillor swimming in his sleep.

'I have no hope that the king's son is alive,' said Sebastian.

'Oh what a great hope you have,' exclaimed Antonio, 'out of this "no hope". Since you grant that Ferdinand is dead, tell me this—who is now the heir of Naples?'

'Claribel, for sure,' Sebastian replied.

Antonio disagreed. Claribel had become Queen of Tunis, she lived leagues away from civilised habitation, and could only rely on the sun for a messenger. It was true she might have a son, but until that son matured enough for his chin to grow hair, there would be no threat to Sebastian's position of heir apparent. So Antonio prodded him further. 'Do you see the good fortune that awaits you?'

Sebastian was beginning to see eye to eye. 'I remember you did supplant your brother Prospero,' he said.

'That I did,' said Antonio, 'and look how well his royal robes suit me. My brother's servants, who were once merely my friends, now obey my commands.'

'And what of your conscience?'

'What of it? A sore on my heel may compel me to put on my slippers, but there must be no conscience in my heart, for it does not move me at all.'

Antonio pointed to the King of Naples, sleeping on the earth he must necessarily return to in death. And this death they could administer—Antonio urged—using only three inches of their unfailing swords. Gonzalo would have to be done away with too; if he lived he would certainly be their greatest detractor. They didn't need to worry about the rest; being courtiers, they would eagerly bend to the wishes of the new rulers.

'You will be my example,' said Sebastian. 'As you got Milan, so shall Naples be mine. Now let us draw our swords!'

'My sword shall fall on your brother,' Antonio told him, 'and let Gonzalo die by yours.'

'Oh but can we have a word—'

But before Sebastian could finish, Ariel arrived again, still invisible to the conspirators. Prospero had foreseen the danger to the king's life, and sent the spirit to foil the plan to murder him. Ariel sang in Gonzalo's ear:

While you here do snoring lie,
Open-eyed conspiracy
His time does take.
If of life you have a care,
Shake off slumber and beware.
Awake, awake!

Gonzalo awoke with a start. 'Angels preserve the king!' he shouted. This broke Alonso's sleep too, who woke up to see Antonio and Sebastian with their swords drawn. 'Why do you two look so fearful?' he asked in dismay.

An explanation was quickly given. 'We stood here watching over your person,' Sebastian said, 'when we happened to hear bellowing sounds. We thought they might've been bulls, or lions even. Did the noises not wake you?'

'I heard nothing,' said Alonso.

So Antonio corroborated Sebastian's report. 'Oh it was a noise terrible enough to frighten a monster, to make the earth quake! There must have been a whole herd of lions.'

But Alonso was still unsure. 'Did you hear the noises too?' he asked Gonzalo.

'I did hear a humming, sir,' he said, vaguely remembering the song Ariel had sung in his ear. 'Strange sounds awoke me, although I cannot be sure what they were. But it is best we stand on our guard with our weapons drawn, or better still, leave this place altogether.'

Alonso was inclined to leave too. 'Let us move,' he said, 'and continue our search for my son.' The coucillor's persistence had revived some hope in him that his son may still be alive.

Ariel watched the scene with satisfaction, and left to tell his master that the king's murder had been prevented.

***

A storm was brewing again. The sound of thunder reached the earth, as Caliban walked laboriously with a burden of wood on his shoulders—another of Prospero's orders.

'May all the germs that the sun sucks up from marshes and swamps fall on Prospero and cover his body with disease!'

he said. Caliban knew the spirits in Prospero's service were always around. When they overheard his protests, they would throw him on sodden ground, make apes chatter at him and bite him, let snakes wind around his body and hiss him into madness. But the tasks Prospero set him were so abominable that it was difficult not to curse.

Caliban was quite habituated with punishment and pain. So when the court jester Trinculo came walking, he took him to be one of Prospero's servants, sent to torment him for being tardy in his work. 'I'll lie flat,' Caliban thought, 'and perhaps he will then miss me.'

Trinculo came talking to himself, expecting the heavy clouds to burst into rain any minute. 'The rain will surely come in thick drops,' he said, and looked for a place to hide. But he found Caliban instead.

'What have we here?' he exclaimed. 'A man or a fish? Dead or alive? What a fishlike smell he gives out! Now if I were in England, I could paint this fish to attract foolish holidayers and earn many a piece of silver. It is common knowledge that Englishmen make their fortune by displaying strange beasts, like the corpses of American natives. But alas, the country's beggars go around with their hands empty.'

While Trinculo continued to muse on the foibles of the English, the storm gained momentum. Finding no other place to hide, he crept under Caliban's gabardine after realising he was an islander, and not a creature of the sea.

'Such strange fellows a traveller must share his bed with under these miserable circumstances,' he said, and waited for the storm to subside.

Stephano, the court butler, had also found himself stranded on this unfamiliar island. He had however made the best of the situation and drunk himself merry. Bottle in hand, Stephano came along, singing what he thought was a despicable tune, and comforting himself by taking large swigs every time it struck him that the song on his lips was one he abhorred.

The master, the swabber, the boatswain and I;
The gunner and his mate,
Loved Mall, Meg, and Marian, and Margery,
But none of us cared for Kate.
For she had a tongue with a tang,
Would cry to a sailor, 'Go hang!'
She loved not the savour of tar nor of pitch,
Yet a tailor might scratch her where'er she did itch.
Then to sea, boys, and let her go hang!

Caliban heard Stephano's tune, and mistook him for another of Prospero's spirits. Fearing punishment, he cried, 'Do not torment me!' This startled the drunken butler. 'Do we have devils here?' he said. Spotting the half-concealed Caliban, he spoke as if to the devil himself. 'Are you playing tricks on me by putting savage Indians in my way? But hey, I did not survive the shipwreck to be frightened by a four-with foul curses. 'May your bodies be covered in blisters!' he shouted.

Prospero promised to punish him severely for his surly behaviour, but no threat was powerful enough to convince Caliban that Prospero's treatment was justified. 'This island's mine by Sycorax my mother,' he said. 'You have usurped it from me.'

When they first came to the island—Caliban recalled—Prospero and Miranda had taken great care of him, fed him berries and taught him their language. Caliban had returned the favour by familiarising them with the island, showing them where the fresh springs were, leading them to the fertile areas and steering them away from the brine pits. But soon Prospero grew intolerant and confined his benefactor in a rocky cave, keeping him from the rest of the island of which he was once master.

'Lies!' Prospero yelled on hearing this. 'Only whips and not kindness can move you to humility. I have treated you with care and lodged you in my own cell, till you tried to ravish the honour of my daughter!'

'And had you not prevented me, I would have peopled this island with many little Calibans,' retorted the slave.

Enraged by this comment, Miranda burst into a diatribe against him, enumerating all the benefits he had made from their association. She accused Caliban of belonging to a vile race, which had made him ungrateful and invite punishment upon himself.

Caliban was not ready to relent either. He thanked Miranda for teaching him to speak her tongue as that had enabled him to curse as well. 'May the red plague put an end to your life for making me learn your language!' he said.

Prospero stepped in at this point, ordering Caliban to fetch them firewood and threatening to rend his body with cramps and aches if he refused. Although reluctant, Caliban was well acquainted with the power Prospero could wield, so he finally deigned to obey his order.

Meanwhile, at another part of the island, Ferdinand was still in mourning, thinking he had lost his father forever to the sea. Ariel observed him in his sad state and filled the air with an enchanting song. It seemed to calm the sea's fury; it soothed Ferdinand's mind. So charming was this song that he couldn't help but follow it till it finally came to a stop.

But before long the music could be heard again:

Full fathom five your father lies,
Of his bones are coral made;
Those are pearls that were his eyes,
Nothing of him that does fade
But does suffer a sea-change
Into something rich and strange ...

'This song is in memory of my father,' thought Ferdinand. 'There is something supernatural about its sound; I hear it legged creature!'

Caliban's gabardine wasn't large enough to cover either him or Trinculo entirely, and both their legs remained visible, leading Stephano to believe that the creature in front of his eyes was an indigenous monster with four legs. So when he heard Caliban speak his language, he was terribly surprised. Enterprising as he was, the butler immediately realised what a fine present this intelligible monster would make for any emperor, and decided to provide him some relief from his fit. He needed the creature to be healthy enough for the journey back to Naples.

This four-legged monster was of course the product of Stephano's delusion, and the fit was actually the false impression the butler had got from Trinculo and Caliban's movements under the gabardine.

Again Caliban cried, 'Do not torment me, I pray you! I will bring your wood home faster.'

Stephano thought the monster was speaking gibberish in his delirium, and decided to give the creature some of his liquor. 'Come, open your mouth,' Stephano said, touching his bottle to Caliban's lips. 'This will put an end to your trembling.'

Trinculo recognised Stephano's voice. He exclaimed, 'But I am certain he is drowned. It must have been the devil who just spoke!'

'Four legs and two voices,' said the butler, hearing a

second voice come from under the gabardine, as the situation grew more and more farcical. 'A most delicate monster! I must cure him of his ague with the help of this bottle.' And he poured more wine in Caliban's mouth.

'Stephano!' Trinculo cried, and this time put all the confusion to rest. 'Speak to me if you be him, and don't be afraid, for I am Trinculo, your good friend.'

'Come forth, if you speak the truth,' Stephano said, and pulled the jester by his legs. 'You are Trinculo indeed! Have you been excreted by this creature of misshapen birth?'

'Oh no, I thought he had been killed by lightning,' Trinculo corrected his friend, 'so I took shelter from the storm under his gabardine. But you must tell me how you escaped the shipwreck. O Stephano, we are two Neapolitans alive!'

Caliban had taken well to the liquor. While the reunited friends marvelled at their survival, Caliban found himself filled with reverence for Stephano, who had provided him with what he thought was a celestial drink. 'I will swear upon that bottle to be your true subject,' he said to the butler. 'Have you come from heaven?'

'Out of the moon, I promise,' Stephano joked. 'I used to be the man in the moon in fact.'

Caliban had grown credulous under the influence of alcohol. 'Then I have seen you inside the moon,' he told Stephano, 'and adored you from the earth. I learnt about you from my mistress, who pointed my eyes in your direction. And there you were, with your dog by your side, and the thorn bush in your hands.'

Caliban's wine-induced deference provided Stephano with great enjoyment, but Trinculo wasn't amused. 'A most gullible monster he is for believing in these tall tales,' he remarked.

But Trinculo's words held no significance for Caliban, who was already making promises to show Stephano every fertile inch of the island and take him to the best springs that flowed on it. 'I will pluck you berries,' he said, 'catch fish for you and fetch you wood. A plague on the tyrant I serve! Never again shall I obey his orders, but follow you instead, O wondrous man.'

'A most ridiculous monster,' Trinculo thought, 'to take a drunkard for a wonder.'

But it wasn't a time to be reasonable when the smell of freedom was so near. 'No more fetching of firewood, no washing of dishes or catching fish for Prospero!' cried Caliban. Then he broke into a merry song, rejoicing at the thought of his imminent liberty.

Ban' ban' Ca-caliban,

Has a new master, get a new man.

Freedom, high-day; high-day freedom; freedom high-day, freedom.

Drunk and misguided, Caliban looked forward to a fresh

lease of life, and led the way for Stephano and his friend, tottering towards the island's delights.

3

There are tasks that are wretched, but if performed with dignity, often such labours bring satisfaction and good fortune. So Ferdinand, under Prospero's orders, carried logs on his shoulders and thought of Miranda, a thought powerful enough to make his task seem pleasurable. 'She is ten times more gentle than her father,' he said to himself.

Prospero had asked Ferdinand to collect a large number of logs and pile them up for him. Watching him toil ceaselessly moved Miranda to tears. 'I beg you, don't work so hard,' she said. 'Set the logs down and rest for a while. My father is engrossed in his books; you needn't worry about him. Let me carry the wood for you.'

But how could Ferdinand let her do such dishonourable work? 'No, precious creature,' he said. 'I would rather that my muscles cracked and my back broke than you go through such trouble.'

'I could do the work as well as you,' Miranda asserted, 'even better in fact, because I am more willing to do it than you are.'

In this way they continued to argue, oblivious to Prospero's presence, who was standing at a distance and watching the scene with satisfaction.

'Let me finish what I started,' Ferdinand told Miranda. 'When you are near me, the night feels like a fresh morning, and my tasks seem less difficult. And yet I am not even aware of your name. Do tell me what it is, so I can include it in my prayers.'

Prospero had asked Miranda not to submit to Ferdinand's requests, but still she told him her name.

As their attraction grew stronger, Ferdinand recalled how he had regarded many women with affection before. But not one of them But not one of them could compare with Miranda, whose every feature was unrivalled.

'I cannot say what features women have beyond this island,' Miranda told him. 'The only woman I know is myself. Nor have I met any man other than you and my father. But I do know that it is only for you I want to preserve my virginity.' But then she remembered her father's instructions and stopped herself short; she had already said much more than Prospero would have liked.

Ferdinand began to speak in turn, and told Miranda that he was a prince, and would never suffer the hardships

Prospero had put him through. But his heart had been enslaved the moment he had set eyes on her, and it was for her sake that he had agreed to undergo those pains.

'Do you love me?' Miranda asked him.

'I do prize and honour you,' he said, 'and my love for you knows no bounds.'

These words touched Miranda so deeply that she began to think herself unworthy of the love Ferdinand had professed for her. 'I will be your wife if you marry me,' she said, 'but if you don't I will die your maid. You may refuse marriage with me, but I will stay by your side as a servant even if it is against your wish.'

'I want to marry you as desperately as bondage longs for freedom,' Ferdinand said, and gave Miranda his hand.

She had disobeyed her father's commands, but Prospero wasn't upset. He had heard the lovers express their sincere feelings for each other, and there was nothing that could make Prospero happier. Things were going according to plan, and his daughter was now engaged to the Prince of Naples. But there were other tasks to be performed, so Prospero returned to his books to make preparations for their union.

***

There was still liquor in the cask. So Stephano swore not to drink a drop of water till he ran out of wine. And he would not let his companions stay sober either. 'Servant-monster, drink up!' he said to Caliban, who still laboured under the impression that Stephano was a demi-god. 'Your eyes are almost set in your head,' the butler continued, noticing Caliban's inebriated state.

'Where else should his eyes be set?' remarked Trinculo, irritated by Stephano's foolish behaviour. 'He would be a valuable monster if he had eyes in his tail!'

But the drunken butler took no notice of Trinculo. 'My monster-friend has drowned himself in wine,' he said. 'But as for myself, not even the sea can drown me. Thirty-five leagues I swam till I finally made it to the shore. Having achieved this feat, I now declare this creature to be my trusted flag-bearer, my standard.'

But Caliban was in no position to stand, his stomach bursting with liquor. 'He could be your lieutenant maybe,' Trinculo pointed out, 'but by no means your standard.'

Trinculo's biting comments didn't please Caliban in the least. 'I shall not serve him,' he told Stephano. 'He's not valiant like you.'

'Ignorant monster!' Trinculo cried, also intoxicated by wine. 'I could jostle a constable if I tried. It is only because I am a valiant man that I could drink such a large quantity of wine today. But you are no man, merely half fish and half monster, and that is why you tell such monstrous lies about me!'

'Oh how he mocks me!' Caliban complained. 'Bite him to death, I pray you,' he said to Stephano.

Stephano told his cynical friend to choose his words carefully. 'If you rebel I will hang you like a mutineer from the next tree!' he threatened.

Now that Trinculo's unruly behaviour had been taken care of, Caliban asked the butler if he would listen to a request. He wanted to avenge Prospero for usurping the island from him and causing him torment ever since. And to this end, he wanted Stephano's help.

Once again Ariel was in the vicinity, and he overheard Caliban. Imitating Trinculo's voice, he said, 'You lie!'

'You lie, you foolish monkey!' Caliban said to Trinculo, while Ariel remained invisible to everyone.

Stephano was enraged by what he thought was Trinculo's insolence. 'If you trouble him any more, I will remove some of your teeth!' he said.

'But I said nothing,' Trinculo promised sincerely.

'And say nothing more,' Stephano told him.

So Caliban continued with his suit. He told Stephano how Prospero had taken the island for himself by means of sorcery. 'Would your highness take revenge on him and get the island back?' he said. 'You will then be its master, and I your faithful servant.'

Having drunk to the bitter end, Stephano was out of ideas. 'And how exactly will we bring about this revenge?' he asked.

'I will lead you to his cell when he's asleep,' Caliban told the butler, 'and you may drive a nail into his head.'

Again Ariel faked the jester's voice and said, 'Another lie! You only make false claims.'

'Give him a few blows, master. Take the bottle from him,' Caliban said, pointing at Trinculo.

'But what have I done? The monster keeps accusing me for nothing,' Trinculo protested and went and stood sulkily at a distance.

With Trinculo standing away from the rest of his group, Ariel could no longer provoke the conspirators to argue amongst themselves. So with no further interruptions, Caliban told the butler that it was Prospero's habit to sleep in the afternoon. While he slept, they would take away his books, without which he was powerless. Stephano could then kill him any way he pleased—batter his skull with a log, stab him in the stomach, or even slit his throat with a knife. 'We must destroy his books,' Caliban repeated. 'By doing so we destroy the knowledge with which he uses his magical implements, of which he has many. And the best of them all is his beautiful daughter, who will become your wife when you are ruler of this island, and produce fine children for you.'

Stephano could not resist such temptations. 'I will certainly kill this man,' he said. 'His daughter and I shall be king and queen, and you and Trinculo my viceroys.'

Fully apprised of the plan against Prospero's life, Ariel made a mental note to report it to his master, as Caliban made merry. 'I am filled with pleasure,' he said, and asked Stephano to join him in singing the song he had sung when they had first met. But Stephano sang a different tune altogether.

Flout 'em and scout 'em,
And scout 'em and flout 'em,
Thought is free.

'That's not the tune you taught me,' said Caliban.

At that moment all three of them heard the tune as if being played on a tabor, but try as they might, they could not locate its source. This was of course Ariel's doing, who was using yet another means to distract the conspirators from their murderous plan.

'Who plays this music?' Stephano asked. 'Show yourself if you be a man. But if you are the devil, d … do what you will. Mercy upon us, for there is nothing we can do to stop you!'

Stephano was visibly afraid. So Caliban tried to console him. He told him how the island was full of unaccountable noises, sweet and delightful, but never bringing any harm. He recalled how various stringed instruments would sound sweetly in his ears, and melodious voices would bring sleep to his eyes. Often while he slept he would see the sky opening up to shower riches upon him. So fantastic were these visions that when he awoke he would long to sleep again.

'A fine kingdom this would prove to me,' Stephano said, moved by Caliban's account.

'Only when Prospero is destroyed,' Caliban reminded him. And before the island's rich offerings could distract Stephano again, Caliban led the way for him and Trinculo towards their enemy's cell.

***

The king's son was nowhere in sight. It had been hours since Alonso and his party had begun their search. Gonzalo's muscles were sore, and his bones ached from walking without pause. 'I can go no further,' he said. 'This island is nothing short of a maze.'

The king himself was seized by weariness. They had searched far and wide, and the little hope Gonzalo had revived in him was dying. So he resigned himself to fate and joined the councillor in resting.

Only Antonio saw an opportunity arising out of the king's exhaustion. He reminded Sebastian of their plan to murder him. 'Do not for one second forget our purpose,' he said to the king's brother. 'Let us execute our plan tonight itself, while they are still weakened by fatigue and thus incautious.' Sebastian nodded his agreement.

Suddenly strange music filled the air. Several mysterious creatures appeared, carrying a banquet. They set the table down daintily and danced a mystical dance around it, inviting the king and his troupe to eat. Then in the blink of an eye they were gone, leaving everyone astonished.

'My good friends, did you hear the enchanting sounds?' Alonso asked. 'Such marvellous music!' said Gonzalo.

Sebastian could not believe his eyes. 'This spectacle makes me think that unicorns do exist, that there are indeed phoenixes in Arabia!'

Antonio was of the same opinion. 'I will believe so too, and every other fantastic thing I've heard before. It seems travellers do not return to their homes to tell lies; it is the fools who stay inside who cannot see any truth in their stories.'

'But if I were to report this incident back in Naples, would the people there believe me?' Gonzalo wondered aloud. 'If I told them of the islanders I saw, mysteriously shaped, yet of manners more gentle than anyone from my nation …'

Prospero, who had conjured the banquet and instructed the spirits of the island to perform the spectacle, watched Alonso and the rest be overcome by amazement. Invisible to everyone, he listened to their remarks. What Gonzalo said reminded Prospero of the treachery he had undergone. 'My brave spirits are certainly made of gentle manners,' he thought, 'unlike some of you present here, who are worse than devils.'

The spirits had vanished, but the banquet remained, beckoning the hungry castaways. Sebastian suggested they taste the numerous dishes that lay on the table.

'Have faith, sir,' Gonzalo said to Alonso when he refused to eat the food. 'In our younger days, we would believe that there were strange people who lived in the mountains with folds of skin hanging from their necks. Or that there were such men whose heads were in their chests. Will you then not eat this food, which lies in front of your very eyes?'

Convinced, Alonso proceeded towards the table, and asked everyone else to follow. But before they could even touch the dishes, lightning bolted from the sky, and out of nowhere a harpy came flying towards them. It hovered right above the banquet and flapped its wings viciously, as the food disappeared just as magically as Prospero's spirits had done.

It was really Ariel who had come in a harpy's disguise, to remind Prospero's detractors of their misdeeds, to make them repent for their treachery. 'You are three men of sin,' he screamed, pointing with his wings at the king, his brother, and the usurping duke, 'whom destiny has caused the sea to belch up on an island which men do not inhabit. And on this island I have driven you insane.'

'You are fools,' Ariel continued, seeing the men draw their swords. 'The excessive courage you display will lead to your own destruction. I and my fellow creatures are ministers of fate; do you think you can stab us with your swords of steel? Put those useless things away and listen carefully to my words. From Milan you did supplant Duke Prospero, and exposed him and his innocent child to the sea. It is this grave offence that has vexed the sea and all its shores and every creature that lives there. For this reason you, Alonso, have lost your son. It is only a matter of time till damnation comes to each of you, stranded here on this desolate island, where life can only be full of penitence and sorrow.'

More thunder sounded, as Ariel in the harpy's guise, vanished in a flash. The spirits who had brought the banquet returned, and taking the empty table with them, they disappeared into the forest.

Prospero congratulated Ariel on his performance. 'Brave spirit, you have followed my instructions to the last detail. And so have the spirits who assisted you. My superior magic has worked its charms, and my enemies are now confused in their fit of temporary madness.' And leaving them in that state, Prospero went to visit Ferdinand and Miranda.

'Oh the monstrosity!' Alonso cried in utter bewilderment. 'The waves themselves spoke to me of my misdeed,' he said, filled with repentance. 'I heard the winds sing it to me, and it was as if the thunder itself pronounced Prospero's name.' Alonso blamed himself for Ferdinand's death in the tempest, and wished his own life would end so he could lie beneath the seabed next to his beloved son.

Seeing the three men in their mad, guilt-ridden state, Gonzalo asked those who were less affected by the recent happenings to stay close to their masters. They seemed to be on the verge of inflicting upon themselves horrendous acts of madness, and after all the terrible things that had come to pass, those at any cost had to be prevented.

4

Finally Ferdinand learnt the reason for the punishments he had had to suffer. His travails were only a test of his love—Prospero explained to him—and he had passed it well. He could now receive Miranda's hand in marriage, and with her father's blessing.

Happy that his hardships were over, Ferdinand smiled at his would be father-in-law. But he had smiled too soon. 'You have received as a gift from me a woman of superior value,' Prospero told him. 'But over time she will outdo even these high praises I sing of her, and then will it be a more appropriate time for you to smile.'

'I have no doubt that she will,' said Ferdinand.

A wedding ceremony was in order, but once again Prospero set him a condition. 'However, you may consummate the relationship only after your marriage is solemnised,' he said. 'If you fail to wait till the rites have been performed, there will be no peace in your lives, only bitterness and hatred, and no children to keep alive your name.'

But Ferdinand was steadfast in his honour. He promised that he would not let anything turn it into lust—no secret cave of the island, nor any suggestion of his imagination. So Prospero left the lovers to each other's company, and summoned his diligent servant.

'What is my next task, master?' said Ariel.

'There is another trick you must perform,' Prospero told him, 'with help from your subordinate spirits. Go bring them to this place, and tell them what their duties are. The betrothed couple expects to see a display of my magical skills.'

A pageant was to be performed, and Prospero explained to Ariel how he had imagined it. Ariel left to gather the spirits of the island and prepare them for the festivities.

Prospero was still afraid that Ferdinand might fail to keep his word and let his passion guide his actions. 'I warn you once more—abstain from taking my daughter's virginity,' he said, 'or you will not be allowed to take your marriage vows.'

'Sir, the chastity of my heart is so strong that it keeps my passions repressed,' assured Ferdinand.

This time Prospero did not doubt the honesty in his words, and called for the pageant to begin.

Soft music played around them as a spirit arrived gracefully, dressed as Iris, messenger of the gods. With great lyrical skill, she welcomed Ceres and Juno to be a part of the celebrations.

Ceres, most bountiful lady, your rich leas,

Of wheat, rye, barley, vetches, oats and peas;
Your grassy mountains where live nibbling sheep,
And flat meads thatched with fodder them to keep;
Your pole-clipped vineyard,
Your seacoast, sterile and rocky-hard,
Where you air Juno, the queen of all the sky,
Whose rainbow-like messenger am I,
Approach as Juno's peacocks fly amain,
Approach rich Ceres, her to entertain.

As a spirit in Juno's guise descended from the sky, another one dressed as Ceres approached, and asked Iris the reason for the festivities.

Iris continued:

A contract of true love to celebrate,
A present generously to estate
On the blessed lovers.

Juno suggested she and Ceres waste no time in blessing the couple. She began to sing a joyful song:

Honour, riches, marriage-blessing,
Long continuance and increasing,
Hourly joys be still upon you;
Juno sings her blessings on you.

It was Ceres' turn next. She sang:

Earth's increase, abundance plenty,
Barns and garners never empty.
Vines with clustering bunches growing,

Plants with goodly burden bowing;
Spring come to you at the farthest,
At the end of autumn's harvest.
Scarcity and want shall shun you,
Ceres' blessing so is on you.

'This is a most majestic vision!' Ferdinand exclaimed, wishing he could live on the island forever.

Happy to see Ferdinand so captivated by the performance, Prospero explained to him how by means of his magical powers he had called on the island's spirits to enact the pageant. And the celebrations had only just begun.

Taking charge again, Iris now called to the nymphs that lived in the brooks and invited them to join in the merriment. Next she invited farmers to dance in pairs with these graceful naiads. In an instant arrived spirits dressed like reapers and harvesters, and each farmer took a nymph for a partner and joined with her in a rustic dance.

Miranda and Ferdinand were enjoying themselves thoroughly. But Prospero had been so engrossed in the celebrations that something important had slipped his mind. Suddenly he remembered that a conspiracy against his life was under way. He exclaimed aloud, breaking the spell, as confusion ensued among the spirits. The festivities came to an abrupt end, and the spirits sadly took their leave and vanished into thin air.

Ferdinand noticed the concern on Prospero's face and

said to Miranda, 'Your father is greatly affected by something.'

'I have never seen him so troubled,' she said in agreement.

Prospero felt that he had upset the couple by ending the pageant so suddenly. He thought Ferdinand looked disheartened, so he tried to console him. 'Be cheerful, sir. The revels had to end sometime. The actors you saw were all spirits, and they have now melted into thin air, just like the fleeting illusions they conjured—the cloud-capped towers, the gorgeous palaces, the solemn temples. The great globe itself will one day dissolve with everyone on it, and like the pageant, leave not a trace behind. We are not any different from our dreams either—forgotten when our time is up, our little lives coming to a close as we fall into the endless sleep of death.'

The pageant couldn't have been merrier, Miranda would soon be Naples' heiress, and reconciliation was waiting round the corner. Yet something troubled Prospero, something inexplicable even to himself. 'Do bear with my mind's weaknesses,' he said to Ferdinand, realising his thoughts had gone astray. 'My old brain is troubled, and I prattle things of no concern to you. If you so wish, retire to my cell and rest awhile. I will take a short walk and calm my troubled mind.'

When Ferdinand and Miranda had left him by himself, Prospero called to Ariel and told him that they must foil Caliban's plan for murder. 'Where did you last see those scoundrels?' he asked.

Ariel had found the conspirators in a state of inebriation.

They were so inflamed by alcohol that they struck at the air for surrounding them and beat the ground for touching their feet from below. Then Ariel had played on his tabor, and charming their ears, led them through trails covered with prickly shrubs, and brought them to a filthy pond near Prospero's cell. Into this pond they had jumped and danced unmindfully, only the putrid water smelling worse than their unclean feet.

Prospero was pleased to hear of their misfortunes. But the drunks were yet to be caught. So he asked Ariel to fetch some gaudy garments from his cell, with which they would decoy the threesome.

'A devil, a born devil,' Prospero said, thinking of Caliban, 'whose nature no amount of nurture can change. The pains I took to teach him to be human have all come to nothing. And as his body grows uglier with age, so does his mind. Now the only thing left to do is plague him and his pesky friends.'

Even while he spoke, Caliban came with Stephano and Trinculo in tow, all three of them dripping wet. Stephano was growing impatient. 'Only a short while now, my lord,' Caliban placated him. 'The prize I will lead you to will compensate for our adversities.'

But losing their liquor bottles in the pond had made the men indignant. 'I will fetch my bottle,' Stephano declared, 'even though I may have to be over my ears in water for it.'

As Caliban pleaded with him to be quiet, Trinculo

noticed the clothes that Ariel had left on the ground. 'O King Stephano!' he shouted. 'Look, a wardrobe fit for you!'

'Leave it be, you fool,' Caliban told him, irritated. 'It's nothing but trash.'

But Trinculo was already trying on one of the gowns. Caliban was afraid the noise would wake Prospero from his afternoon sleep. 'If we run out of time, that cruel sorcerer will turn us into barnacles and apes!'

Stephano and the jester paid him no heed. They heaped the garments on Caliban's arms and ordered him to carry them to the place where they had stored their wine. 'Or I'll turn you out of my kingdom!' Stephano yelled drunkenly.

He only stopped to listen when the shouts of hunters came to their ears. The spirits had taken the shape of hounds, as Prospero and Ariel set them on the threesome. Seeing the dogs come after them, they ran helter-skelter.

'Fury! Tyrant!' yelled Prospero to the dogs. 'Grind their joints and cramp their muscles. Make them more spotted than mountain cats!'

As the chasers and the chased disappeared into the distance, Prospero sighed. His enemies were at his mercy. Soon Ariel's labours would come to an end and he would have his freedom. There was only one thing left to do.

The time had come for the revelations.

5

In the linden grove near Prospero's cell, the King of Naples sat dismayed. His brother Sebastian stood with Antonio, still dazed from their encounter with the harpy. The rest of the entourage despaired of their situation, and tears ran down Gonzalo's cheeks as he watched the king in his maddened state.

'They're prisoners of your spell, master,' Ariel reported to Prospero. 'If you saw them now, your heart would surely soften.'

Though their crimes and treachery had filled Prospero with vengeance, he believed it was nobler to forgive. 'With the wrongdoers repenting for their misdeeds, my cause for revenge has ceased to exist,' he said. 'Release them, Ariel. It is time I lifted my charms and restored their senses.'

Prospero prepared to reveal himself to his friends and foes of twelve years past. With his staff he traced a circle on the ground. He called out to the elves that lived on hills and in the brooks, the fairies that made ringlets in the grass under night's cover, and the spirits that rejoiced at the curfew hour whose bell declared them free to roam the earth till the sun rose again. To these helpers Prospero said, 'With your aid I have caused the sun to eclipse, made tempests roar, rifted trees with thunderbolts. Sleepers from their graves have risen in answer to my magical spells, hills have quaked in response. But today I vow to relinquish my power, to break my staff and bury it deep in the earth, and drown my books in the sea.'

Music played as Ariel came, drawing the king and his men into the circle. Prospero observed them after all those years, as they stood charmed, unable to see or hear him. 'Bring my hat and rapier from my cell,' he said to Ariel, and the airy spirit returned with the items in a trice. Prospero disrobed, and for the first time in twelve years he appeared in his ducal attire. He then sent Ariel to the ship to wake the master and the boatswain and bring them to him.

By this time the spell had broken, and Gonzalo, finding himself able to speak again, wished some heavenly power would guide them out of the frightening island.

But they found to their horror that they had unknowingly entered a magical circle which held them captive. Prospero came before them and said, 'Behold the wronged Duke of Milan!'

The king's party stared at him in disbelief. For assurance's sake, Prospero embraced the king and welcomed him with cheer.

'I cannot tell if you are Prospero or an apparition that has come to haunt me,' said Alonso, mustering all the courage he had. 'But you seem to be made of flesh and blood. And since I saw you, my afflicted mind has healed.' Alonso asked to hear the explanations behind all the strange occurrences they had recently witnessed. But before anything else, he would have Prospero tell him how he had survived all these years and on that island.

But the story could wait; first Prospero owed the kind councillor a debt of gratitude. He held Gonzalo in his arms and said, 'So great is your heart that its honour can be neither measured nor confined.'

Next he addressed Sebastian and Antonio and told them he had received knowledge of their plot to assassinate the king, and he could bring down the king's anger on them if he so wished. But luckily for them, his intention was not to punish.

With Antonio's treachery still fresh in his memory, it was difficult for Prospero to call him brother. Yet he forgave him, and told Antonio that he had no choice but to return the dukedom as its rightful duke was still living—even the king had so decreed.

Alonso could still not bring himself to believe that the Prospero before him was real. 'Share with us the details of your survival,' he demanded. 'Tell us by what coincidence we have met, as it has been only three hours since we were shipwrecked upon this shore and the cruel waters claimed my son.'

Prospero said he had lost his daughter too, but unlike the king, he had patiently accepted his fate.

'A daughter?' It had been so long that Alonso had forgotten Prospero had a child. 'How did you lose her?'

'I lost her to the same tempest that you were in,' said Prospero, as it was the storm that had brought Ferdinand to the island, where he met and got engaged to Miranda.

Prospero noticed that the other men were still staring at him in amazement, thinking their eyes were deceiving them. So he told them yet again that he was indeed the duke who was deported from Milan, who landed on the shore of this island to be its ruler instead.

But he would share no more, as his story was not one meant to be told over a meal, but a chronicle to be narrated over days. So he welcomed the king into his cell and promised to delight him as much as he had delighted Prospero by returning him his dukedom.

Alonso's delight knew no bounds when he saw Ferdinand, alive and well, sitting inside Prospero's cell and playing chess with his betrothed.

Once again Alonso could hardly believe his eyes. 'If this is only an illusion, my one son I will lose twice.'

But Ferdinand had already seen his father at the mouth of the cell. Overcome with happiness, he came towards Alonso and knelt.

'You have all the blessings of an overjoyed father,' said Alonso, helping him up. 'Now tell me how you came to this island and made the acquaintance of this maiden.' Like his son, even Alonso mistook Miranda to be the island's goddess.

Ferdinand corrected him. 'She is mortal, sir, but by immortal providence she is mine.' He told Alonso that he had chosen her for his wife without his father's permission, thinking him to be dead. 'She is daughter to the famous Duke of Milan,' he continued, 'of whom I have often heard but never saw before.'

Guilt-ridden for having unknowingly made his future daughter-in-law suffer, Alonso asked Miranda for forgiveness. 'Give me your hands,' he said to the couple, 'and let those who do not wish you joy suffer grief and sorrow.'

Joy was in the air indeed. 'Such wonderful creatures there are in this world,' Miranda exclaimed on meeting for the first time in years so many of her kind.

At this point, the master and the boatswain arrived, eyes wide with wonder. 'Look!' cried Gonzalo. 'There's more of our party! Hadn't I prophesied that this boatswain could never drown?'

The boatswain was glad to be reunited with the king and his men. He informed them that the ship was safe in harbour, as splendid and seaworthy as when it had first set sail. He told them how every member of the crew had found himself asleep under the deck, and was wakened by shrieks and howls and the sounds of jangling chains. And then in an instant he and the master had been separated from the rest of the crew and brought magically to this place.

'Well done, my diligent spirit,' Prospero said to Airel. 'You shall have your freedom soon.' Pleased to hear this, Ariel left to find Caliban and his companions and bring them before his master.

There were still two men missing from the king's company. Prospero pointed to Stephano and Trinculo, as Ariel returned, driving them and their new friend on.

The alcohol's effect was wearing off. Caliban took in the sight in front of him, and thinking the men to be wonderful spirit-friends of his master, realised Prospero was indeed powerful. He feared he would be severely punished, pinched to death even, so he vowed to be obedient and asked Prospero to have mercy on him. 'What a fool I was to take a dull drunkard for a god,' he admitted.

Prospero introduced Caliban to the king as the deformed son of a witch who could control even the moon and the tides. He told Alonso of this creature's plot to take Prospero's life, a plot in which the king's servants were his willing accomplices. 'And since you would like me to take pity on you,' Prospero said, turning to Caliban, 'go to my cell with your companions and decorate it nicely.'

In this cell Prospero requested the king and his party to rest their weary minds and muscles, and promised to relate to them the story of his life since he came to live on the island. The next morning he would take them to their ship, and everyone would return to Naples, where Prospero hoped to see his daughter and Alonso's son wedded.

To this end he made a sincere promise. 'You may now look forward to calm waters, favourable winds and a journey so smooth that soon we will be sailing next to the royal fleet from which you became separated.'

And after this final task did Ariel get his liberty, Caliban his island, Ferdinand and Miranda each other, Prospero his dukedom—and if this formidable duke were to be believed—everyone else their just deserts.

Supplementary Reading

Character Sketches

PROSPERO

With his awe-inspiring stature, his expertise in the magical arts, and the power he wields over almost everyone in *The Tempest*, Prospero is undoubtedly the play's central character.

Early in the play we learn that Prospero's dukedom has been usurped by his treacherous brother Antonio. At this point Prospero certainly earns our sympathy, banished from his own state to live on an unknown island with his three-year-old daughter. While Antonio turns Prospero's followers against him, we come to know that he isn't entirely successful, that Prospero did have at least one loyal supporter. On the night of Prospero's banishment, the old councillor Gonzalo secretly furnishes him with food, clothes and the books he valued above everything else.

When Prospero reaches the island, the only thing at his disposal is his knowledge of sorcery, an art he had dedicated all his time to, naively trusting his brother with the governance of the duchy. But Prospero learns from his mistake, and on the island where he comes to live, he is relentless. According to Caliban's account, in his early days on the island Prospero used him to his advantage, and later enslaved him by means of his magic and proclaimed himself ruler of the territory.

Although Prospero denies most of Caliban's accusations, we are never sure whom to believe. In fact, Prospero's plan of revenge, the sufferings he makes King Alonso and his men undergo, and the painful punishments he metes out to Caliban, do not paint a favourable picture of the wronged duke. While he takes pride in his own magical skills and considers them harmless, he can only cast aspersions on Caliban's witch-mother Sycorax, and decries her for being able to control the moon and the tides. Prospero wants to avenge his brother and the king for taking his dukedom through unlawful means, but never feels guilty for having usurped from Caliban the island that rightfully belonged to him.

By the end of the play however, all issues are resolved. Antonio is compelled to return to Prospero his dukedom, Ariel is freed from his service, and Caliban is master of his island once again. Prospero has a change of heart—instead of seeking the revenge he had initially planned, he forgives everyone and looks forward to Miranda and Ferdinand's wedding, which suggests his desire for a harmonious relationship with the King of Naples who was once his enemy.

Throughout the play, Prospero betrays qualities both agreeable and otherwise, and it is this indeterminacy of his character that makes him one of Shakespeare's most significant creations.

CALIBAN

On multiple occasions in the play and from multiple characters we hear that Caliban is a deformed savage, a creature only half human, whom it is easy to abhor. It is established time and again that his appearance is ugly, and his mind equally detestable. Miranda tells Ferdinand that he and Prospero are the only two men she has ever seen, thus refusing to acknowledge that Caliban is human. To Trinculo and Stephano he is nothing more than a useful monster, a strange islander who will make for an exotic gift to any emperor in Europe.

But Caliban corroborates these claims only partially. He does not deny that he had attempted to rape Miranda, but he never makes a clear admission either. He does wish to murder Prospero, and with Stephano and Trinculo hatches a plan against his life. But it is clear that this is his reaction to the years of punishment Prospero has made him suffer and the hateful tasks he constantly performs under his master's orders. Caliban's murderous plan and his constant curses do not logically indicate an innate vileness, even though that is what Miranda would like to believe.

Caliban also mentions the various ways in which he came to Prospero's aid when the latter first set foot on the island. And although he is not repaid in a gracious way, Caliban is incredulous enough to repeat his acts of kindness when Stephano pours wine in his mouth, which intoxicates him into believing that the drunken butler is a 'wondrous man', a demi-god. Once again we are led to believe that it is his inclination to trust strangers too quickly and not a race-induced evilness that causes Caliban to suffer punishment, slavery and exploitation.

MIRANDA

For the better part of the play, Miranda is depicted as an innocent, wide-eyed girl, guided completely by her father, who engineers her first meeting with Ferdinand and ensures that she falls in love with him. In relation to Miranda, Prospero is very much a conservative patriarch; twice he warns Ferdinand against taking her virginity before their marriage is solemnised. In turn, Miranda, by being engaged to Ferdinand, unknowingly ensures that Prospero's enmity with Ferdinand's father, the King of Naples, will end. In this way she becomes Prospero's vehicle for achieving one of his chief objectives. Miranda thus serves two main purposes—of a useful daughter, and a beautiful future wife who will guarantee the continuance of her husband's and her father's lineage.

But there are instances in the play in which Miranda comes across as forthright instead of submissive and docile. She goes against her father's commands and meets Ferdinand secretly. She even reveals her name in spite of

Prospero's warnings. Assuming her father to be asleep, Miranda asks Ferdinand to let her do the task Prospero had ordered him to perform. And when Caliban jeers at them, Miranda harangues him for being ungrateful, paying no heed to the codes of decorum women of her time were expected to follow.

Even though her acts of assertion are far outnumbered by the instances that show her to be the epitome of chastity and womanly goodness, Miranda, like her father, remains an ambivalent character.

Questions

1

a. Who is Gonzalo? Why does he think the ship he is on will not sink in the tempest?
b. Who has brought about this tempest? What does he say about his past to his daughter?
c. Why does Ariel think he should be freed from his master's service? From what torments had his master freed him twelve years ago?
d. Who is Caliban? What reasons does he give for the displeasure he feels towards Prospero?
e. Why does Ferdinand agree to follow Prospero's orders? Why does Prospero want to punish him?

2

a. Whose loss is Alonso mourning? What does Francisco say to comfort him?
b. What do Antonio and Sebastian plan to do while the rest of their group is asleep?
c. If Gonzalo were king of the island he is stranded on, how would he govern it?

d. Why does Sebastian blame Alonso for their current situation?

e. What does Caliban promise to do for Stephano? Why does he think Stephano is a 'wondrous man'?

3

a. What has Prospero ordered Ferdinand to do? How does Miranda plan to relieve him?

b. How does Miranda go against her father's wishes?

c. What does Caliban promise Stephano if he killed Prospero and became the master of the island?

d. When Stephano feels afraid on hearing Ariel play on his tabor, how does Caliban comfort him? What does he say about the island?

e. What does Ariel, in a harpy's disguise, say to the king, his brother and Antonio? What is Alonso's reaction?

4

a. Why had Prospero been punishing Ferdinand? What does he offer him as a reward?

b. What warning does Prospero give Ferdinand? What is Ferdinand's reply?

c. Which are the three goddesses that play a part in the pageant? What does Prospero suddenly remember while the pageant is still in progress?

d. What does Prospero tell Ferdinand after the pageant has ended?

e. Where and in what condition had Ariel last seen Caliban and his companions? How do Ariel and Prospero chase them away?

5

a. After calling out to the spirits of the island, what does Prospero vow to do?

b. How does Prospero appear in front of Alonso and his men? What does he do to assure Alonso that he is indeed the wronged Duke of Milan? What is Alonso's reaction?

c. Why does Prospero praise Gonzalo? What does he say next to Antonio and Sebastian? Does he forgive them?

d. What does Alonso do when he finds out that his son is engaged to Prospero's daughter?

e. How does Prospero introduce Caliban? What does he ask Caliban and his companions to do for him?

f. What promise does Prospero finally make to Alonso? What do you think Prospero will do once he returns to Italy?

About Shakespeare and his Plays

WHO WAS SHAKESPEARE?

William Shakespeare (1564-1616) was an English poet and playwright. He is now widely regarded as one of the greatest writers in the English language and the greatest playwright of all time.

Shakespeare was baptised on 26 April 1564 in Stratford-Upon-Avon. His father John was a glovemaker and dealer in wool. His mother Mary was the daughter of a prosperous farmer. They had eight children.

In 1582, Shakespeare married Anne Hathaway. They had three children, Susanna, Hamnet and Judith.

Little is known about Shakespeare until 1592. At this time, records show that he was living in London and writing poetry. His early plays were also written during this period.

In 1592, Shakespeare became a founding member, actor and playwright of the Lord Chamberlain's Men, a theatre company. The most famous actor in this company was Richard Burbage, who played the roles of characters like Richard III, Othello and Lear. This company was later renamed the King's Men.

Little else is known about Shakespeare's life, though he clearly earned a lot of money for his plays. He became a substantial landowner.

He died in 1616, and was buried in Stratford.

In 1623, two actors from the King's Men had Shakespeare's plays published in what is now called the *First Folio*. This contained thirty-six plays and was sold for £1.

The period during which Shakespeare lived and wrote is now called the Elizabethan age, during the reign of Queen Elizabeth I (1533-1603), during which many great playwrights, such as Christopher Marlowe and Ben Jonson, wrote.

The works of Shakespeare that survive include thirty-eight plays, 154 sonnets and two long narrative poems. Shakespeare's plays have been translated into every major language, read, performed on stage and made into films, and continue to inspire new interpretations all around the world even today.

WHY READ SHAKESPEARE?

'Shakespeare's work is the fullest expression of the dilemmas that we as humans face ... he's capable of seeing two sides of a situation so there's always drama and there's always conflict.'—Michael Boyd, RSC Artistic Director.

Shakespeare is still read and loved because his plays contain fabulous stories and wonderful characters, and are full of marvellous poetry.

Shakespeare's plays are best watched first and then read, because in performance they take on a new magic. Today many filmmakers are making films on Shakespeare's plays. You can try watching them to get a sense of how the plays would be in performance.

PLAYS AND THE THEATRE IN SHAKESPEARE'S TIME

Performances in Elizabethan theatres were very different from when you go to see a play now. The actors and the audience always interacted. Shakespeare's company had to perform against the noise of the crowd which shouted, threw fruits and tried to join the actors on stage.

Unlike the playwrights of today, writers like Shakespeare would have to present their theatre company with their ideas. The leading actors and managers would decide whether they liked it or not, and only then would the playwright proceed. This close relationship meant that the playwrights often wrote roles with a particular actor in mind.

When a play was completed, actors would receive only their lines, and not the whole play. Thus, until rehearsals started, they would not have any idea how the parts would fit together to form a cohesive play. Rehearsals were used to sort out all the details not mentioned in the script, such as songs, exits and on-stage actions.

The Elizabethan stage was different from the proscenium stage we see in theatres nowadays. The cheaper tickets were for the groundlings, the audience on three sides of the stage. The more expensive tickets were for patrons who sat in covered seats further back. The stage was covered in straw. The wall at the back had three entrances. Above the stage was a trapdoor for lowering performers down to the stage, and on the stage itself was another trapdoor for surprise entrances and exits.